Tongue is a Fire

Books by L. Sydney Abel

Gruvel the Great
Ish-ish Ishbochernay
Keypya and the Pirates
Kingsley and the Spider
Marge and the Wobbly Onkey
Mr. Runkin's Secret
Patrick Duck
Smelly Nelly Welly

Timothy Other:
The Boy Who Climbed Marzipan Mountain

The Evergreen Wolf

Tongue is a Fire

L. Sydney Abel

SPEAKING VOLUMES, LLC
NAPLES, FLORIDA
2021

Tongue is a Fire

ISBN 978-1-64540-449-1

For Karen

Portraits in clouds navigating the sky
Deep in the blue where dreams arise
Parachuting thoughts
Catch and imagine

Δ

For:
Norm, Dunc, Mick, Shaun, Ron, and Les

Shapes become Animation
Heroes are brought together
Passage is earned to The Criminals
One of the Waiters–forever

Δ

For:
Demons and Angels
and all the broken-hearted people,
and all the dead who gave their input–they know who they are

Δ

Transcend

Front cover:
Inspiration from Aboriginal lore
A being called a Quinkan is such a powerful supernatural spirit

Method by the Author

Emotive words come from anything that sparks my attention. Words don't perceive self-pity; they spout emotion at that time. Passion written is better than thoughts festering, as they say 'Better out than in'. Words are not meant to hurt in any way. If anything, they are there for constructive rehabilitation. They are a form of self-exorcism if anything.

I write my novels in character–much as an actor upon set–and that is no different when it comes to searching out feelings. It often turns out to be extremely spiritual, a kind of feeling tarot. I've learnt so much about myself from this method. I feel more openly sensitive.

My emotive words can be read as they are–just words–or interpreted by an emotional state that fits, or misunderstood to arouse controversy.

It is possible to learn a lot about yourself from meandering thoughts put down as emotive words.
I've learnt:
I'm the light; I'm the dark–in equal quantities. I can be that light at the end of the tunnel and, at times, the bogeyman.

Whatever the observer sees for him/herself is fine by me, C'est la Vie.

Foreword

In lunacy of it all
Poetry is the most subjective form of expression
Dark and light writings from meandering thought
I call them Emotive words
No boundaries
No categories
Words are set in an unconventional style
That's me all over

There's a lot of the paranormal surrounding my writings.

The progression with anything I create goes through its criticism stage. I am my biggest critic, and always will be. I step away from my work after I think it's complete. Then, when the mood takes me, I re-visit. If I still have creative excitement, then I work with it until I feel going any further will drive me insane–In lunacy of it all.

Stick by your convictions. But never think you are the best at what you do. Simply run with them. We are all stardust.

Your belief and views are your own. No-one should dictate otherwise.

So on that held assumption: Never dictate your views upon others who don't see things your way. Never offend anyone who has a dissimilar opinion. We are all different. We are not sheep. We all have our own ideas of what the world should be like. Live and let live.

Don't take umbrage to what follows. They are my thoughts into words. No one can make me think or say otherwise.

Embrace the freedom of speech. Like it or not, we all have something to say.

Table of Contents

Sentenced

When I'm Dr. Jekyll
　　I'm not Mr. Hyde
And when I'm Mr. Hyde
　　I'm not Dr. Jekyll
Which me is being fickle?
The confusion of decision is for the mood to decide
Do me the kindness Hyde
　　and plan suicide
I'll be right by your side

Last Stand in the Corridor

I would like to mention some things which happened in the establishment known as school. They are not important, but have scarred my attitude towards those unusual creatures known as teachers. I often wonder if life is inescapable of the things which mark you. I say this because of my aversion to education. How profoundly ironic: I married a teacher. Love is blind.

Let's rewind time to November 1974; it's life-changing for me. I'm in the sixth form at Kingston High School, doing A-level art over one year rather than the two. I'm also taking technical drawing, as I did the previous years–a great aid in learning the discipline of composing drawings which graphically communicates how something functions, or is to be fabricated.

Everything was going smoothly until the head of English stopped me in the corridor.

She told me to attend all her lessons or leave school. In other words, show up or be expelled.

I never liked school; the look on this female teacher's face brought closer the reason why. Her stance portrayed dictatorship. Her shadow draped over me like I was an ant under a stamping-down shoe.

I explained how some of her English classes conflicted with my art classes, stating someone–not actually saying it was her, but arguably meaning it–was at fault and clearly should have seen I couldn't be in two places at once. Being condescending isn't wrong when you know whatever you say won't make the least bit of difference to someone obstinate. I say obstinate because this teacher knew I didn't need English to get into art college–she was in no way putting my future first. She wanted it all her way or not at all.

She told me to give up art. Those were her last words. Not literally, but they were as far as I was concerned. With an order there was to be no compromise. She walked away with a spring in her step. I felt like I had lead boots on. I was crushed.

Dictatorship doesn't work with me. I trudged to the person who knew me well–he'd been my form teacher, my metalwork teacher, and still my technical drawing teacher.

I described my ordeal, with fury.

He understood my feelings as he knew my intentions of becoming a display artist–with hopes of working in the television and film industry– or a graphic artist. He explained English, along with Maths, took priority in the curriculum. I felt his failure to help. All the way through my school years I believed him to be the only teacher to really teach me anything. Thank you, Mr. Harrison.

Plead your case at the top, I thought. *Go see the main man in his closet/office.*

My previous close encounter with this arrogant shit was shortly after a friend was lectured for something he'd done out of school. This headmaster wanted to see me. He clarified my friend made advances towards another boy. Saying this boy's parents weren't happy about it. They implicated I knew about it and didn't want gossip.

He's gay isn't what I'd say.

The head stated my friend was homosexual, and bluntly asked me if I was homosexual.

I was stunned at his bigoted audacity. I looked him straight in the eye (no pun intended) and spat my denial. I stated that I found his insinuation offensive. I naively felt I needed to defend myself. I stated who I had as a friend was my concern, arguing I'd known this friend since I was five and been told his leaning. I rightly pointed out he'd never hidden it. Saying that he flamboyantly flaunted it, adding that I'd seen him in a dress, heels, and makeup (I smiled in the face of disapproval), adding, why on earth should that bother me? If he wanted to make advances towards another boy then C'est la vie. I finished with; whatever a friend tells me is in confidence. I then walked out of the headmaster's office and in justice to his attitude slammed the door, as if in his face. This headmaster was obviously homophobic or in denial of his feelings– the prick.

Needless to say my plea fell on another obstinate dictator.

I went to see my art teacher–the open-minded. Art was the least important subject to every other teacher. I knew he couldn't help, but he needed to know the situation. At least his reaction was on my side–he was gutted. He asked if he could keep some pieces of my work. I felt honoured.

As I've said, I hate being dictated to–I walked out of school, with my satchel over my shoulder, got the bus to the city centre and steered my way to the careers office. I knew there was no chance of an apprenticeship beyond the age of sixteen. Here endeth being taught art.

Let's rewind time a little further; it's September 1973. English classes introduced me to poetry. The teacher–female, attractive, hippy, with big round tinted glasses–asked if she could put some of my words she found favourable into the next school poetry magazine. I'd no reason to deny her.

When the magazine came out, my wordy pieces were nowhere to be seen. I saw her after class. I remarked how good a certain page in the magazine was, adding, I didn't know the lyricist to a top ten album was a pupil at this school. I pointed out he'd used a pseudonym.

She looked confused, so with an apology promised my work would be in the next issue.

I told her not to bother and take a walk down the yellow brick road. Here endeth my interest in poetry. I was rash. On reflection; I thought poetry rather girly. Pity the fool.

Forward time to December 1974; I became an apprentice television engineer, with one day plus night at college for the next four years; studying radio, television, electronics, and mechanics.

The following years witnessed my interest in playing music. I learnt bass guitar, joined bands, and discovered song writing.

Lyrically, my words became my feelings; depressed, happy, screwed up, you name it–emotive words I call them.

Older emotive words: They project periods in my life. Some seem so penitent while some still take how I feel today–very strange.

Newer emotive words: These are my perception of the world today. We live in hope of transcending to a better place.

Images/Illustrations: Art never became what I intended it to mean to me. I now illustrate for my children's books. I use many mediums, including the computer (a useful tool). All illustrations begin on paper.

My last art teacher gave me a serious piece of advice. He told me any art you create must have a title or it has no meaning. The point was taken.

I can't forgive those who could have helped but chose not to because of rules or prejudices. They are the ignorant; they have not given me their values. These are my memories, my thoughts, and my opinions.

The Darkest Room is in Your Head

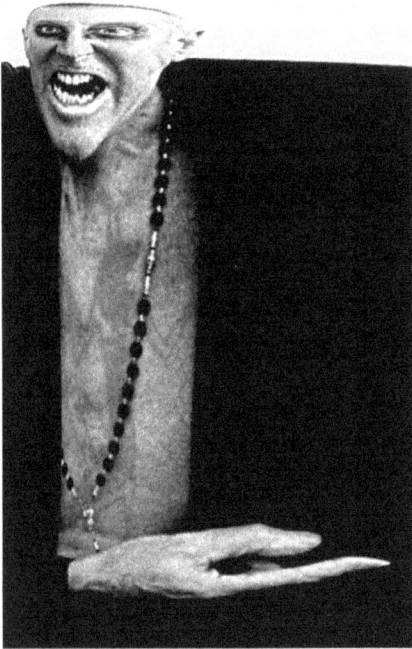

Demon standing there…

The darkest room exists
    waiting silent
Delays in resist
    mordant
Thoughts…
    and the snake takes you there
Belief in all bestial waits
    beware

The Lightest Room is in Your Heart

Angel standing there…

The lightest room is real
  let it shine
Struck anvil
  someone's lifeline
Thoughts…
  and the ladder takes you there
Belief in all divine awaits
  declare

Tongue is a Fire

The tongue cannot be tamed
It is an uncontainable evil
    full of noxious poison
Holler to the depths of hell
    when your tongue is a fire
Quench your verbal abuse
    drink the water given
    beneath the sun's rays
Look for sunlight on cold water
Speak loving words or be dumb
    control that tongue

Let Us Part

Your servitude plays my attitude
Take yourself from my mood
We all sin
    so let's begin
I stand before you completely nude
Take yourself from my heart
    and let us part
We have no feud
My heart has an open door
    so leave
Evermore

Life's a Play with Unforeseen Extras

From the book: Timothy Other: The Boy Who Climbed Marzipan Mountain
Chapter 46: It was there so it wasn't a dream–stick of resolution

Persons represented:

Timothy, *orphan at the Dreams and Hopes Orphanage.*
Mr. Penny, *a ghost.*

Timothy pulled and pulled, until his face was red. The stick didn't budge; it was frozen solid in the earth. Timothy turned towards the house and looked up into the upper windows. Mr. Penny's office was dark. 'If you are ever in need of me when you are here, I will always be in my study.' The words seemed to float in the air, ringing bells only Timothy could hear.

Scene – *The forlorn office.*

Enter Timothy *and* Mr. Penny.

Mr. Penny. Hello, Timothy.

Timothy runs into Mr. Penny's arms crying, Uncle!

Mr. Penny. You can only see me because your need is so great. Do you understand?

Timothy shakes his head, he is holding too tight to think.

Mr. Penny. I am here for you as I promised, but only so you can understand a little more.

Timothy. I can't pull out the stick. It's stuck.

Mr. Penny. There's no need to. There's nothing there but a stick.

Timothy. Why did you put it there?

Mr. Penny. So you would know it wasn't a dream and that *now* is very real.

Timothy. Will you always be here?

Mr. Penny. The time will come when it will become impossible for you to see me. But that doesn't mean I'm not there.
    Remember, Timothy, (Ghost and voice growing fainter)
    think of the people you've already helped in life,
    think of all those others whose lives you will touch,
    think how worthwhile your life is and will always be.

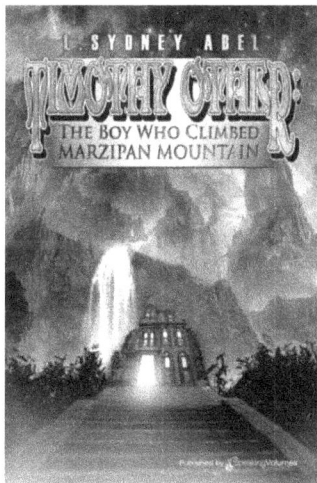

The Room of Truth

The Messenger's face was full of surprise–he'd expected supreme wonder. What greeted him was restrained horror. To him, the room was as evocative as a crypt–the walls were of stone, the ceiling arched as in a church. The wall of skulls was breathtakingly beautiful in its macabre simplicity. Skull upon skull looked upon the room's guests. Each look bequeathed love of faith. The 'room' was first and simply a place for the initiated. The 'truth' was in its literature, and that combined made its magnificence.

The Custodian decreed to 'The Room of Truth': "My breath is in the wind. Upon my calling of your name, you shall come and be worshipped. You are the darkness from which there is true light. You are no longer the fallen, but the risen that will shine upon all who follow. Your light will engulf us all."

A black, shapeless form slipped from the table and like a serpent crossed the floor. When it reached The Custodian it stood as a man, naked and with horns–decaying black flesh filled the air with the stench of death.

Excerpt taken from the book:
12:07 THE SLEEPING

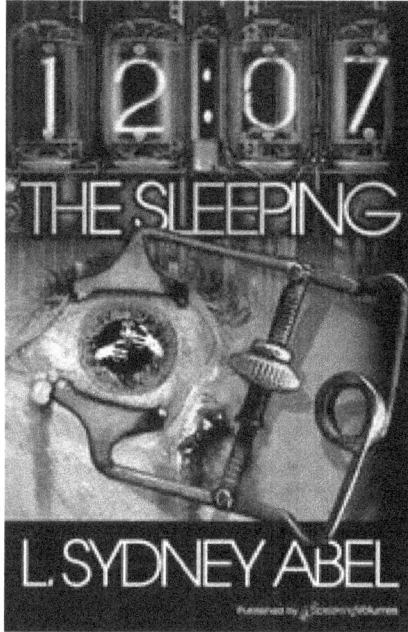

I've always been interested in the paranormal.

It's undoubtedly because of the time a phantom walked out of the wardrobe.

I was five.

I screamed my lungs out.

I call those phantoms The Sleeping.

Death's Lament Speaks

You fool
    behind that protection shield
    you wield words of fire
    in your mood's desire
But time is only a period your breath hangs onto
And so
    to me you'll come
    the unwanted one
    when you give your last breath
I–Death
    will embrace you
    will take you to the abyss
    where your soul will be tormented
    and kept for all eternity
You are paradise's mistake
    for me to take

Rooted in the Unconscious

Wane Barecell was an unreasonable by profession or so Wake Elmsjar would say when he got the chance, which just happened to be every day.

"You're unwanted," said Wake, "don't you forget it. You have grandiose delusions."

"You're one to talk," replied Wane, in a mocking manner, "and that unwanted, raggedly-shawled thing died at seven days old."

"I'm not dead!" cried Wake, shutting down for the day.

The room was cavernous. Darkness oozed from the walls, the ceiling, and the floor.

The next day:

As it often did, a spark lit distance in starlight.

Wane played the game. His instruction to Wake was confident, "I'm not talking today. I'm busy. I'm being creative."

In your head you can be anything or nothing. Today be somebody, for tomorrow you may be nobody.

A-Haunting They Go

Navigation from their world to mine
A-haunting they go
    from the wardrobe door
Bond by 'own will' is the guideline
Their visit instigating war
I fight the good fight
I will finish life's play
Even if I'm alone in the footlight
The love given I will not betray

Self-Exorcism

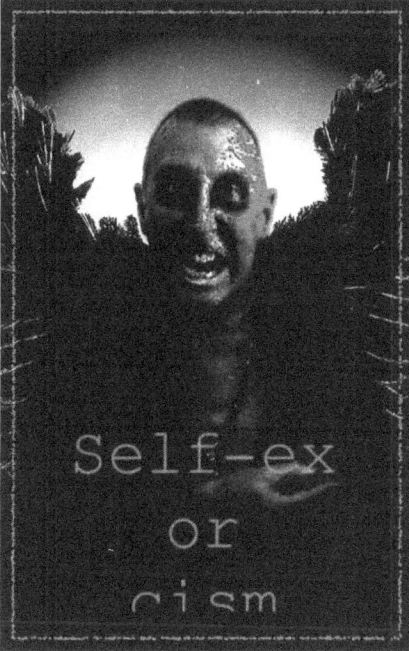

They were about him like a thick fog
They were the walls
    the ceiling
    and the floor
Tell the story
Put it in a work of fiction
Self-exorcism
To the underworld guardians
    known as The Sleeping
    my soul is not for reaping

In All That Love Demands

I've seen them on tops of buses
Holding hands and looking like lovers

I
I've screamed away my dreams
I've hurt in doing so
I must forgive my means
In my veins flows sorrow

I say I had to try
Pouring out my exertion
Those in darkness heard my cry
I pray in their subversion

I say to the unwanted
That I understand
How souls are created
In all that love demands

You
I've heard you whimper in nightmares
I'm your protector
We've common shares
Aren't I your director?

I say you're wanted
You're all I need

Your wounds I've salted
With love I feed

I say as we grow older
Hold my diamond hands
Together we shoulder
In all that love demands

Don't fear dreams that can't happen
Just be happy in all you've achieved

Memento Mori

All are clowns in life
    to be sages in death
There will be no funeral service
    only interment of ashes
Listen to the preacher's words
    as the urn is placed in the ground
No music played
    only thoughts sing of happier times
It is a wish
But first
    remember that I have to die
Death's wings veil my eyes
    his blooded bill kisses my nose–life foreclose

Balance

Does life have balance?
There's good
    there's bad
There's happy
    there's sad
Body death
    bodily re-entrance
There's doubting
    there's clairvoyance
Does life have transience?
There's young
    there's old
There's warmth
    there's cold
Body living
    bodily decadence
There's spiritual
    there's quiescence
Does life hold talents or silence?
They're calm
    you're enraged
They're free
    you're caged
Body dead
    bodily annoyance
You're fighting
    they're flamboyance
When the Sleeping come

When the Sleeping Come

The Sleeping came into the room like the Schutz Staffel
    this was no protection party
It was Nazi SS looking their decaying worst
    whose all-black uniform was designed by Death itself
Masked white faces
    carrying soulless searching eye-sockets
    advanced towards the unwanted
They all belong to Hell

Rats

We move through life at such a
     head-pulling and squashing pace
     that we need to slow down
It's not a race
We are not rats

See things–understand things
     no matter how small
     the entire shebang has intention
One day we will be whole
We are not rats

Life's not a treadmill

Likely Thoughts

Rats

Every conceivable horror lurks within imagination
Let miseries leave and disappear through your bodily wall
    like rats from a sinking ship
Let your soul be free
See things differently
    ascend into harmony

Evil to the Core

The reflection in the mantelpiece mirror was exquisite
Clothes worn were faultless for the occasion
    the cuffs of a shirt were showing below the sleeves
    of a black jacket
Cufflinks caught the incandescent light from many candles
A smile into the mirror returned belief

Another smiled before the mirror–breath warmed its nearest soul
Reflection of loveliness
    with eyes of green had a gift for tempestuousness
The devil will take me for what I'm about to do
Replications watched one another

Soon there will be carnage
Eyes of the superfluous see nothing
    whereas passion sees the gory-dead as vivacity

Of the Dead

I see you falling
    I hear you calling
There's only violence
    physical vivacity
Hold to your interfaith
    you sinner
It's not my place to forgive

Kissing you deadly

Design of Virtues

The heart is like the moon

Sometimes the heart shows love unmeasurable
  sometimes it shows naughtiness pleasurable
Other times love thickens for the greater
  other times for the lesser–thin water
Occasionally the heart shows love for the realm above
  occasionally it blackens for the domain below–end of
Love craves for its opposite creation
  love craves for the same formation

Holler at the moon

Don't misconstrue your virtue
Rendezvous with design

Moon Waltz

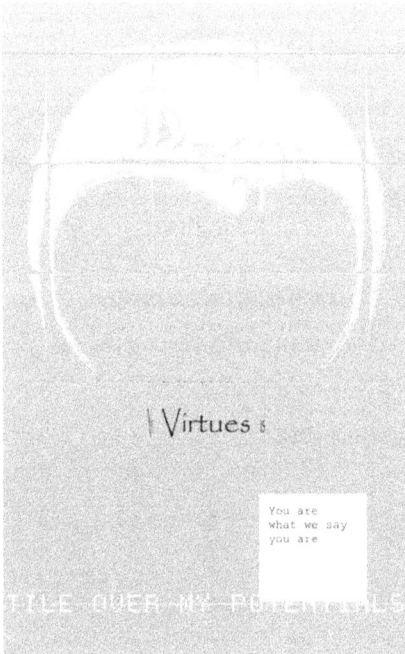

Moon years slowly started to conceal the most enchanting
creature imaginable

She was ageing
    salivating gems from her lower lip while eyes burned
    flame
Her skin became wrinkled in a palette of grey
Charcoal-bruised deep creases quickly crevassed
Blood boiled in their depths
    spitting time in creation
She was after all a living entity
Love is bestowed upon us
Love embroils us all

It's My World

This is what I've been searching for
This is what I can see
The hills move out of distance
As the world turns round me

It's my world
Yes it's my world
And it's turning round
  turning round
  my world

The best we can hope for
Is living and loving free
All I can believe in
Is the swaying palm tree

Now it's me calling for you
You want all I can see
Now the hills are hiding the view
Shake your head at me

There's always another headstrong
Blind to obedience
You bore the stubborn
To be spirited in resilience

It's my world
Yes it's my world
And it's turning round
    turning round
    my world

Another One

Sitting there
    on the table rather than chair
Tells of self-determining
Let's be fair
    never a sovereign
But a king all the same

Cold in New York

It was cold in New York
It had just started to snow
The first time I saw you
    you were all alone

We were just friends
No it ain't that way at all
    we were just friends

Have you ever tried saying goodbye?
It's easy at first
But the more you do it
    the pain just gets worse

When I left you that night at Joey's bar
They were all putting their arms around you
And I can still see the light in your eyes
I thought you were gonna cry
Remember those flowers I brought you
They were such beautiful colours
I think that's the way I'll always see you
So alive
    yeah!
So alive!

We were just friends
No it ain't that way at all
     we were just friends

The Killing of Mr. Green

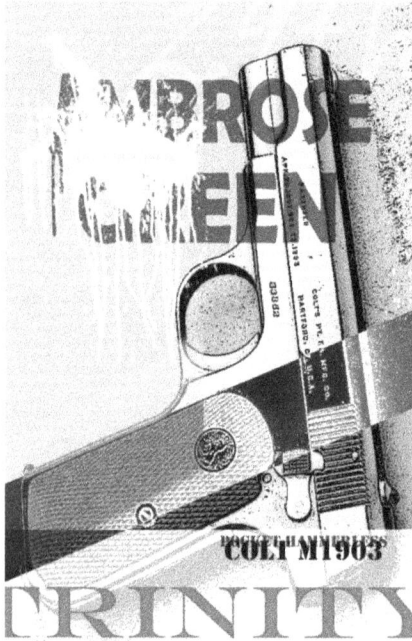

During the great crash of 1929 and on the thirteenth floor of
a building
    where an office window looked pleadingly upon Trinity
    Church
    a calm man with nothing left to lose gently pulled open
    the right side desk drawer
From it he took a Colt M1903 Pocket Hammerless
He placed it into the roof of his mouth
    and unceremoniously blew his brains out
It was Black Tuesday
October 29th

Throwing Pebbles

Throwing pebbles on the water
     is a pleasure I desired
See the ripples now growing
     is my mother still alive?
Watching the daylight now dawning
     is a feeling of my guilt
See the child now–he's grown up
     a man just like his father

Times pass
     memories linger on

The musing has to decide
     who laughs and who cries
There's no feeling of emptiness
     there's no feeling of being deprived
There's shyness in front of people
     it's one thing you can't explain
Is there a reason to my depression?
     Will I see my mother again?

Sunlight on cold water

I See

Dream
    a slice of life
Cut with a surgical knife
A name
    written thereon
A journey to embark on

The pain in my heart tears me to pieces
And I hope my dreams never show
    that I wanted you before
And all the ice in the world
    can't keep my temperature low
Darkness in skins creases

Don't Feed Out of My Hands

You can stand alone in church
    and say the things you believe in
But don't bedevil me with your solutions
I've my own evil

Don't feed out of my hands
Feed out of your own

See the sickness in my brain
    share its lonesome remorseful pain
But keep it to yourself
Don't succumb to fear

In this moment of truth
    take a look at your hands
We're all full of tell-tale signs
Breaking down and crying

Being blessed with God's gifts
    helpless in the fact of not knowing
These difficult times will pass
When it's a new phase

And is every God a reasonable God
    or not at all?
The truth comes with the light
Vanquished the moon

Don't put your life in my hands
Your life is your own

The Scar

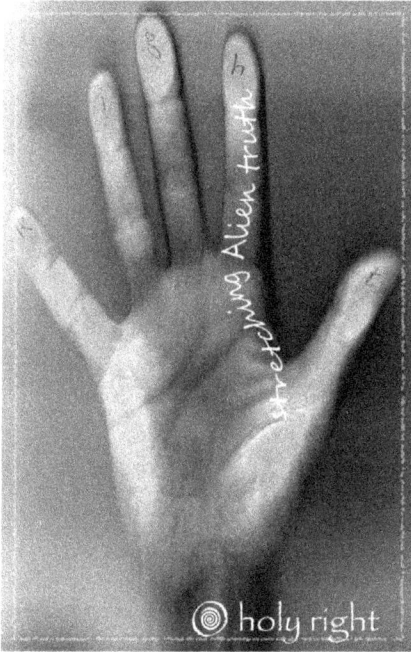

O holy right
    the wrist is gaping
Letting light into its depth
Shooting joy
Celebrating

One Good Friend

I'm packing up my thoughts tonight
I'm going up into the mountains
When we sail away
    ain't it blue just like the ocean?
Little children they never say
    what will you be today?

What you doing down on your knees?
Are you praying for another day?–Oh Lord!
This is the journey
    like new memories they've just begun
There are no more welcomes
    and the taste of you is still so sweet

I remember I had one good friend
Kept on saying 'Don't say grace'–Oh no!
She won't let you do
    exactly what you're thinking
There were words I once thought to say
    ain't it strange I've thought of crying?

Oh my sister
    what you gonna do?

The Mansion

We lived at the house in the photo, fondly referring to it as The Mansion, for 9 years. I wouldn't say the house was haunted, but there were strange happenings–lights being turned off and that sort of thing.

My wife is adamant that someone tucks the sheets in on her side of the bed. That someone is affectionately referred to as 'the bed-tucker-inner'.

It would appear that we were being haunted. Utter nonsense, or was it?

It should be noted that when we climb into bed, we always pull the sheets and covers out from under the mattress. Also, my wife is always first out of bed. This must be clearly understood or nothing frightening will come of the story I am going to relate.

This haunting became a regular event, but mostly while we slept. 'The bed-tucker- inner', in no way upsets my wife. Strangely she liked it, she found it comforting. I didn't. I found the idea that someone walking about our house, coming into our bedroom, and tucking my wife safely into bed, gave me the shivers. I refused to believe it.

My sightings:

One night, on climbing into bed and kissing goodnight, I turned to go to sleep. My wife straightaway said 'I've been tucked in'. I turned and looked, and indeed she was tucked in. I was still not convinced.

One morning, when I climbed out of bed for work, my wife–being on holiday, which allowed her a lie-in–calmly said 'I've been tucked in'.

I looked, and I have to say it terrified me. The sheets and covers where hospital-bed-made. I was now convinced. I was a firm believer.

When we moved from The Mansion, it seemed 'the bed-tucker-inner' didn't come with us. Now whether the haunting was for my benefit or my wife's, I cannot say. But what I do know is that the people who bought our house only lived there a month. The residents after that, to my knowledge, are still there.

The Bed-Tucker-Inner

House on the hill
    has a bed-tucker-inner
Kindly spirit who never harmed
    whose heart you warmed
    and never alarmed
Maybe you walk still
    and tuck someone else in
If indeed you are a ghost
    it's my wife who misses you the most

For Aunt Minnie

Hand on heart
I've no reason to deceive
Just believe
Let memory start

My knowledge of my dad's family is virtually unknown. What memories I have had to be dragged from his remembrance. He had his reasons why he didn't speak about them, but I'll never understand his reluctance to tell me about his life.

I don't recall meeting anyone but his mother Mary Jane and his sister Minnie. I can recollect how poor my grandmother was in comparison to my other grandmother, who seemed to live like royalty (thinking on that, she did some very similar things to the Royals–those skeletons in the cupboard things).

Minnie was my dad's favourite sister.

My dad described his sister's situation. She was living in a two-up, two-down terrace house, unfitting for inhabitation, or for the use of better words, a slum–pest-ridden.

Minnie was in poor health when she came to stay with us. She took my bedroom. I don't remember seeing her at all at meal times.

My dad was fighting tooth and nail with his family and the council on his sister's behalf.

Unfortunately her health worsened and she was taken to hospital.

On one of his visits he found her dead in bed. No nurse noticed her passing.

I recall the anguish my dad suffered. I don't recall Minnie's funeral. I do recall strange happenings thereafter.

Ouija board:

Contacting the spirits is one thing I'll never do again. Whoever it was that came wouldn't let me out of my bedroom, no matter how hard I turned the handle and pulled. I was terrified. I screamed. I kicked the door. I stamped the floor.

Then, miraculously, the door opened.

I leapt down the stairs, two at time, and bounded into the living room. No-one heard my screams, my kicking, or my stamping. Worse than that, no-one believed me.

Levitating:

It's not something I've practiced; I wouldn't know where to begin. I can distinctly recall my body rising from my bed; strangely my feet remained on the bed as I swung 90°. I hung there looking at my feet. I wasn't frightened in any way. It was pleasurable. I felt distant from everything. If my feet weren't my anchor I might have drifted away.

My flight ended as I swung back and lowered. It was such a strange sensation. Had I died? Was it Minnie holding me down?

There were instances in my bedroom when I felt I wasn't alone. But that could have been my imagination, couldn't it?

Years later my children would stay at their grandparents. They feared my old bedroom. I'd never told them about Minnie or the happenings.

R.I.P. Aunt Minnie.

Minnie

Our house–my room–she came to stay
    until illness took her away
Alone she gave her last breath
    her rattle given to the angel of death
In a hospital bed she lay lifeless
    eyes sightless

A soul of niceness
    seeks the whiteness
She left the ward
    with the one she called Lord
How long had she lain dead?
    A pillow supporting her sweet head

A Corner for Fools

Feeling sad and lonely
Well ain't it strange?
Feeling cold and hungry
So you feel the same?
Empty and alone
Well ain't it strange?
I ain't got a friend
So you feel the same?

Say
They say
They say we're all really crazy

I've painted eyes
        in every colour and size
I was close to you
        I hope you realise

There's a corner for fools
Well ain't it just me?
This corner's for real
A real friend in need
Sad as a clown
Paint a face for me
I've done all my crying
Am I as mad as can be?

Say
They say
They say we're all really crazy

Fools End

Restrained
    until…
You can never blot out what cannot be forgiven
Au contraire
Unto the angel I confess

Talking Times With Gods of Heaven

Genesis 1:26 And God said
    Let us make man in our image, after our likeness…

Why did God speak in the plural?

From the story of Genesis
    my teacher will tell me this
Who are the men of the stars?
Talking times with strangers

Without giants and other sons of gods
    I'm primitive and at odds
Who are we lest we learn?
Talking times with strangers

A lesson with no speech to receive
    trying hard to hear to believe
Who are we listening to?
Talking times with strangers

Someone holds secrets and spills contradictions
    I'm praying we make transitions
Who are starving without the gift?
Talking times with strangers

How can the grass grow green
    when we know no grass grows?

Is destruction within everything?
No flowers in spring–the indecency of time

Time is its own seed

Nana and Pat the Dog

My great-grandmother told the story of how her son had been a dispatch rider during the Second World War, and of the day she believed he died: She was upstairs when she heard her son call from the kitchen 'It's only me, Mother'. She ran down the stairs to find no-one there. It was then she heard a loud crack. She discovered the wardrobe mirror had cracked. Later she found out that her son had been killed. She was convinced he'd visited from the beyond.

The Curse of Tide

In through the door
   and across the floor
'It's only me, Mother' was called
Down the stairs came Mam
Then as if in a film:
The mirror crack'd
Death came before the telegram

We're Not Talking

There's a fire
    that burns inside of me
It rages when we're not talking
I don't know a thing about you
Really I don't
    I'm thinking of you

We could watch
    a new day dawning
We could see the ships setting sail
I will whisper 'I want tomorrow'
I need to see you
    before the day ends

We're not talking
We're not talking
I'm waiting
We're not talking
We're not talking
I'm missing you

I will follow
    I'll follow you everywhere
How I wish you were here by my side
We could talk–forget our pride
I want tomorrow
    with you

Horse Staith (oss wash)

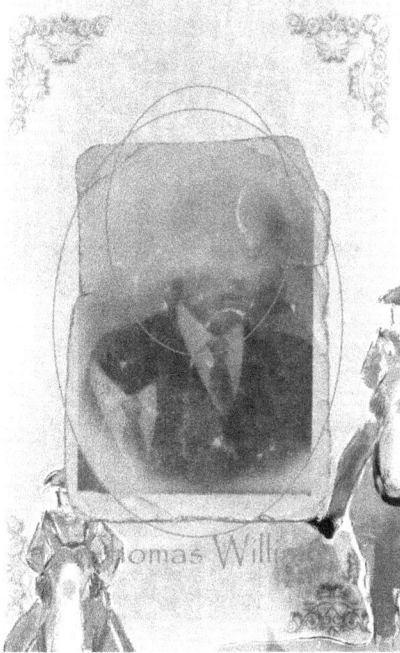

You were never to know me
Sentence reciprocated
I was designated
    celebrated
Often manipulated
    detonated

Cry You Cry

I've seen you crying
    but I've never seen your smile
Holding your love for fear of falling
    so I can call this the last time
And in the next day
    those bells ring out on a Sunday
Placing your picture in a gold frame
    won't make you an angel–it won't change you

What would you do
    if I told you?
I didn't want to hold you
I didn't want to see you
I think you'd cry
    you'd cry
    you'd cry

There's no way of escaping
    don't you know it's my heart you're breaking?
Breaking my heart over you
    I'm a broken man when I'm not with you

The Soul Spook

They scorn
  then crown you with thorn
Eyes haunt the voyeur
The soul spook
  as in the gospel according to Luke
Why eat and drink with a sinner?

Saturday 11th December 1926: A Fay speaks to her chosen one.
Vivi kissed the cheek of the one she called hers. "Who'd ever imagine how your love for the divine would diminish when your soul met mine? Don't be governed by society or God. Let your soul be free as it was meant to be. My soul has yours as yours has mine. Surely isn't that enough?"

Falling

The blue moon's gonna shine away
    the blue moon's gonna shine

Don't call on the broken-hearted
Don't tell me things to comfort me
The words won't touch in the right places
    run among a million flowers

Falling
    forever touching wishes
Falling
    while we sleep
Falling
    shower me with kisses
Falling
    love is deep

Now your smile is breaking through
Sometimes you have to hold on me
And your touch is reaching in
    pin down the clouds and cover me

Torture the small who wonder
When the blue moon shines away
See through the words
    wait for the beasts to come out to play

Two Oranges

Oranges
    from the lady who understands
No discrimination in her smile
    love from rough hands
Oranges
    oranges galore
I cannot remember anymore

One of the Waiters

Hey there brother
Did you go out last night?
Are you one of the waiters?
Yeah! You know–a waiter–that's right!

Hey there sister
Bet you went out last night
You don't waste time with the waiters
You got better things to do with your time

Hey there lady
I hope you get what you're looking for
It was never this good in Paree
You know our love just happened to grow

One thing I get from you
You make me feel good at night
And I'll keep on loving you
And if that's all right with you then that's alright

Random Waiter Thoughts

An error worth taking: Life seems more than this: There's elegance in China: Holding a passion: My heart couldn't turn: I'm a loser: Always been fooled: I've seen ravens in numbers: You dissolve my life: Time ran out: Walk away in silence: Fascinating old stories: In a course of several turns that anyone can make–think on…

The Prophesy

I was called to come and listen: My wife was standing on the Mansion's landing, just outside our bedroom door.

I was halfway up the stairs when she said 'Nora is going to die today'.

'Did you dream it?'

'No.'

That evening, after work, my father phoned to say that grandma died today.

Truth Thieving

People come and people go
Some have faces that you know
Countless lives are inglorious
    some notorious
    some victorious

There are those that are worlds apart from a godly heart
There are those that are venomous creatures
A few rage war with the mindless more
As others take refuge in lobotomy procedures

Brain inflicted with sharp words
Truth thieving from our affords
Lies carved into believing
    thoughts leaving
    thoughts weaving

Not partial to being cemented in influences by others

Run

When I was young
    nothing was fair
I think I've changed
    won my wings and ran away
It doesn't seem right
    all this fuss about who gets the daylight
You never can tell
    round in circles–such a beautiful sight

Run
    run
    run
    run
    run

Though I can't read
    I talk to people who want to talk to me
And they tell me stories
    which I hear once and I want to hear again

Like some lonesome traveller
Kick the dirt from your shoes
I was waiting for him
He never came–though I looked all day

Oh I got confessions
    about the time I stole your jewellery and things

And I prefer not to tell
    about the time I stole your love

Confessions

A free spirit's kiss
> upon a white neck
> sent a scarf of feathers to fall softly over breasts
> and gather between legs
It was then she felt the goodness of heaven enter her
> and warm her soul
The nightmare was forgotten
> it simply dissolved from all thought
All fears wiped away
> to darkness they'll stay

Heaven Can Wait

Heaven can wait
You decide–don't make me cry this way
Want something–you want it too much
Goodbye to the kingdom that I love

I know
    and you know that it's true
You know
    and I know that it's true

Endless–endless days
There's a warm wind which blows
From time to time you can smell the jungle
And your hands rest in pockets of water

We were together
There's a blood-spattered door in my life
And autumn burns in your throat
As the beat of your heart whispers

I know
    and you know that it's true
You know
    and I know that it's true

Bloody Door

A figure of woebegone stumbled through an unlocked door
    into a room of dying-ember darkness
What crime will you deny?
Don't be tortured by your losses
Heaven's souls can open doors directly into our world
    through dreams
      if you let them
Knock!
Knock!
Who's there?

My Values Change

I have dreamt
    of the dreams of far away
I have seen
    the Moulin Rouge dancers
I have heard
    all's fair in love and war
All the same
    it's tempting to leave

I've been told
    new cities are made from gold
And it's true
    life ends with the open hand
And it's said
    for those who wait
It comes in time
    and I may leave

My values change

Sand on sand
    a mirage across the desert
Heart rules head
    can often be suicide
Seen from above
    everything looks flat

L. Sydney Abel

When it's over
    I can leave

Lonely cry
No one to hear you
Fallen down
No one to catch you
It's all over
Thanks for the memories
It's all so strange
I'll try to change

My values change

Red Sails in the Sunset

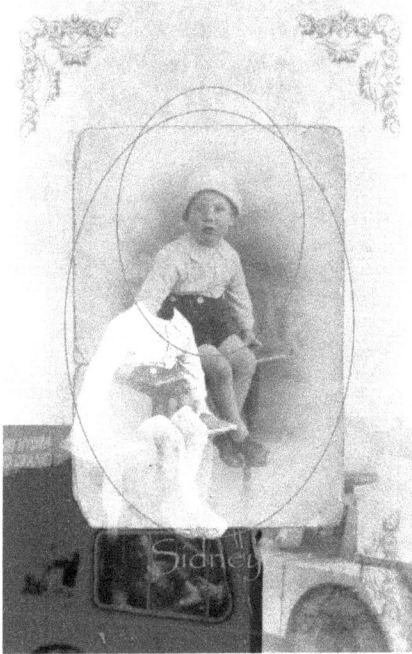

A table to sit on
    then later under
Singing 'Red sails in the sunset'
Regret
    mindset
Life's an alphabet
    with voice
        thundering and lightning

In the Morning

Should have kicked the ass to its knees
He told you living was a gift only for kings
Keep your fingers crossed
Nothing
     no nothing
     will ever change
Here comes the beating sun
Emptying its message of love
Tears are for the never-never
Hope lies
     waiting
     in the morning

In the morning
     you can travel
In the morning
     when the sun is low
In the morning
     you can travel
In the morning
     take your bed and go

Movies of the coast and the burning cross
Hold tight as your fingers glow
Give another place another time
Watch the traveller
     see things

you didn't know
When there are no eyes watching over you
And the air is sparked in fear
No strength of pride and hope
One man
and his dreams
are broken

The Traveller

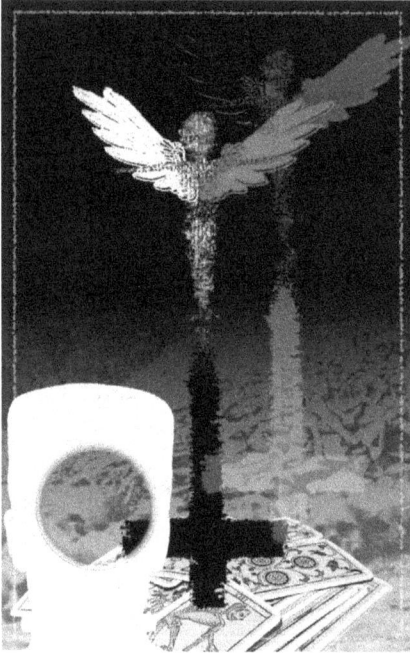

Race through room after room
    always searching
    never finding
Cold dark rooms
    empty rooms
    nothing rooms

Who Sent Red Roses?

One simple blue room
    one simple red room
I don't know whether I'm coming
Don't know whether I'm going
Always following suit for you
    following suit for you

I'll swim the ocean
    I'll climb the mountains
I'll follow you everywhere
Through rain and through snow
Always following suit for you
    following suit for you

Who bought you those flowers?
    Who sent red roses?
I've just got to know
I don't want to sound jealous
You know I'll follow suit for you
    I'll always follow suit for you

I told you I could murder
    it would be a crime of passion
I'd do anything for you
If only you'd want me to
Always following suit for you
    following suit for you

You See

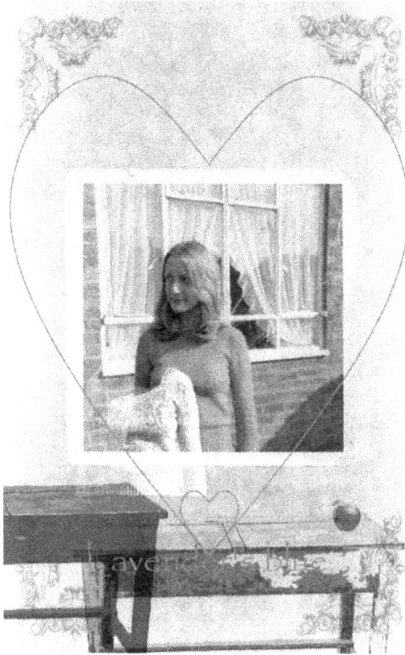

Waiting is nearly over
The sand beneath your feet
    blown by time
The path to choose is mine
Intensity has chosen the spiritual unknown

Home to You

To cure the blindness
is not by opening the windows
See the sun at night
put wine on my feet
Say it more than once–Sit down! Shut up!
How many times
to understand the truth

I'm coming home to you
home

How much of this
upsetting state
Don't want any prayers
or an angel at dawn
The face of the sun can erase your face
I'm hallucinating
I'm seeing all

I'm coming home to you
home

Burning with love
through new eyes
It's me and it's you
as it should be
Rub out my face to leave no delusion

L. Sydney Abel

I'm the mistake
I'm the illusion

I'm coming home to you
home

Judgement

I'm the hue of the coldest lake
For pity sake let me see all you've seen
The air I intake is from your dream
Visit me again
      stand by my side
love allied

The Spy Who Came in From the Cold

Take the city
    take the lights
Take the music
    take away what's nice
I don't want to be associated with this anymore

Everybody's
    making fun at me
Everybody's
    saying I'm crazy
I don't want to be associated with this anymore

Across the courtyard
    away through the door
Away to freedom
    and who knows
I'm the spy who came in from the cold

Too many cities
    too many lights
Too much music
    too much of what's nice
I'm still the spy who came in from the cold

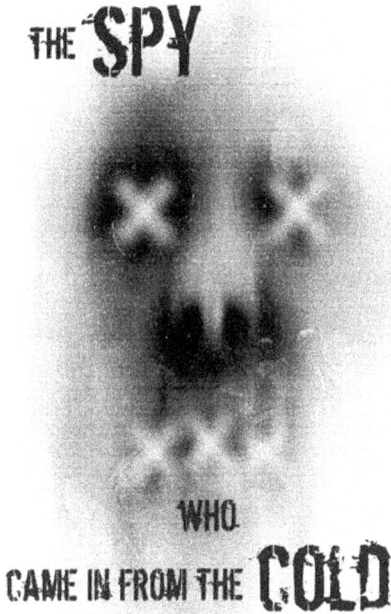

Can I really comment on what I can't see?
Words
     they're my undoing

The Blue in Your Eyes (for Karen)

Always seen the blue in your eyes
Before the day I held your hand
Always wanted to look at you
Always my dreams expand

I blow you kisses each sunrise
From my 'with you' dream
Your skin is my compass
You're a voyage to redeem

When you're in my arms
And I squeeze your life
I am you
    you are me
    rust I
    rust you
Husband and wife

Precious Stardust

Precious stardust
heaven sent
Morning star
evening star
leading light
Soul bright
Heart content

Lift Up Your Hearts

And when the sky turns red
    from the fires burning
And the lights are out over Israel
    and the ships are silhouetted waiting

I'm gonna take you
I'm gonna take you
    away from this

Blind eyes look upon you
    in a void ignited with horror
Strength is built of arrogance and faith
    and a newborn's cry fuels succor

When all excuses are exhausted
    we stand tall on the horizon
Children are mothered and cared for
    and life's revolution is rising

All I know was they belonged
    as my edges melt into loss
The mention of a King stayed
    and I too shall believe in the suffering cross

We are blinded by dreams

Blinded by Dreams

The future is never what it seems
    when blinded by dreams
Suffer the little children
Deity takes and deity gives
Souls wait to be reunited again
    ask the divine to explain

So young

Criminals of This World

Criminals of this world
      will take everything
Those heads of state
      playing ruling

Princes in tower
      palace or prison
Declared illegitimate
      criminal arisen

Crowned the third
      princes slain
War of the Roses
      all in vain

Infamous
      evil tyrant
      child murderer
      twisted King
Wanted was a stiff feather
      on bastard wing

Mad King under car park
      barking mad criminal
      Isn't death a lark?
Lunacy is principal

Mad King

Bow wow
       woof
       woof

"March on…
If not to heaven
then hand in hand to hell."

William Shakespeare – Richard III

Holding My Breath

I've been close to death
But I can't remember just how close
I've seen death from both sides now
I'll hold the cards I chose

I'm going down
    I'm holding my breath
I'm going down a long way
    I'm holding my breath

I've played the game your way
Life doesn't come in sevens
Watching life pass you by
Is my idea of a life sentence

Why does it seem there's no release?
Is it right to go through this pain?
How can life be so cruel?
Everyday hurts just the same

Up Close

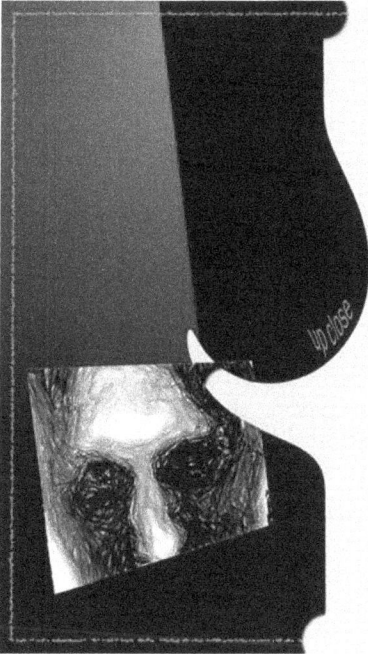

It was darker
     almost gloomy with all the doors closed
I feel someone has recently visited
     they've be up close and kissed
The wrist's jagged white line is still visible
     reminding how neighbouring was death
Never close your eyes to the real world

Innocent People

I saw the blood
    flowing down the street
I saw a man
    crying at another man's feet
I saw flesh
    torn from my arm
I saw the rich
    hiding safe from harm

Don't bring the walls crashing down on me

A politician
    was calling people around
A woman
    sobbed for the dead on the ground
A man
    stood with his back to the world
A thief
    took as death unfurled

What was the reason for this to happen?
Why the suffering of innocent people?
Could it be their time has come?
Could it be time has ended?

Don't bring the walls crashing down on me

Innocents

Biscuit boy stand amongst kin
    dirt covers skin
To be shoeless through pride
    poverty you can't hide
To see with your eyes
    from my disguise
Forever your son
Explain to him
The innocent

The Call of the Wild

Waiting for the snow to go
    the call of the wild
But mother I don't know
    if I'm still a child
I don't want to leave–really
    it's the call of the wild

It's calling you
It's calling
    it's calling
It's calling you
The call of the wild

Taking the risks is all part of
    the call of the wild
Learn from courtly love
    show worship compiled
The taste of wine is like
    the call of the wild

Find answers to questions
    from the call of the wild
Open eyes to suggestions
    don't hide those reviled
Life hides danger in shadows
    hear the call of the wild

It's calling you
It's calling
    it's calling
It's calling you
The call of the wild

Ghostly Encounter

A few months after my mother passed away I took the family to the seaside resort of Scarborough. It was a reminiscence sort of day–we talked of the woman we loved. I remember sitting in glorious sunshine with my father next to me. I was people watching. There was an old lady sat opposite, enjoying the sun and the sea air. I didn't respond to her smiling face. When I turned to her again I was being watched by an apparition of my mother. I stared until fear made me look away. I turned and looked again. My mother was still there. Her image lasted about four minutes. Finally she faded away, leaving the old lady to smile at her surroundings. I didn't mention what I'd experienced to my father for fear of upsetting him.

Gipsy Wild

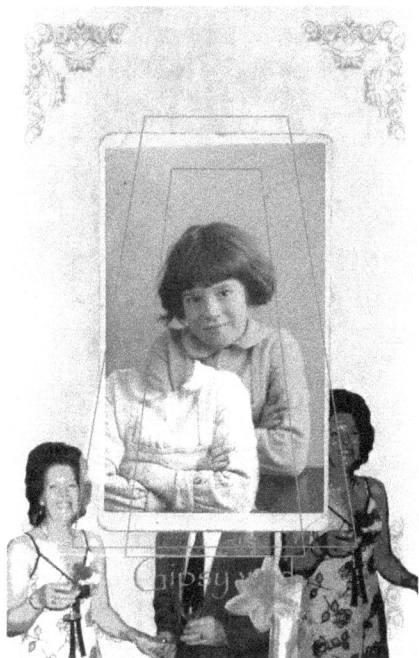

Given wild to her world
To be tamed
Maimed
Beauty unfurled

Fall in Line

Then
The tongue had the power of life and death

These soldiers
    want you to fall in line
These soldiers
    will give you time
Time to die in file
Time to die at no rank level

Time
    falling time
Time
    you fall in line

A silent kiss
    to death in advertising
Your country needs you
    solute comprising
Who wants to die the Unknown Soldier?
Who wants to die? Fall in line

Time
    falling time
Time
    you fall in line

Tongue is a Fire

Now
The tongue has the power of life and death

Someone somewhere
    should take the blame
Once in charge
    of a warfare game
Whose life can they play with now?
All guilty puppets fall in line

Time...

Freedom of speech is worth fighting for
The individual shall not be repressed
    their voice needs to be heard
Say no to big brother
We are substance dissolved in a given solution
    but who are we?

Desert Rats an' All

Weep
        let the tears fall around your feet
The colour of death doesn't suit you
        its hue is like the coldest lake
Wish my tears to freeze
I would have begged on my knees
        your death differently

One Leopard

Is that a way
     is that any way to talk?
You've got a psychic mind
     and a left hand deal

Take a card
     take my advice
The one in the middle
     will do you right

One leopard
     stalks
     from behind
One leopard
     cries
     from behind

Ask the questions
     ask the questions of life
There's no correct answer
     who then cares?

So many paths
     so many paths to take
If you take the wrong one
     then that's your mistake

One in the Middle

Roll up
      roll up
      it's come to pass
Why divide
We cannot hide
Our attraction to other bodies–gravitational mass

Words for You

It's hard being away from you
It gets lonelier and lonelier each day
Trying for new horizons
I miss you
    no matter what you say
Ever tried grasping the darkness
    watching the darkness slip away?
Waiting for the moment
    when there are no words for what you want to say
Would you say I was foolish?
Would you put your lips to mine?
Stars will keep on shining
    well beyond our lifetime

The Moment

Ghost
      under my ceiling
      my brain is defining

Time
      are you in mine
      or I in yours?

I need a third party
      Teddy
      why is she carrying flowers?

No Pleasures

Had enough of this world we live in
An orchestration of voices shouting
    'we've got the power'
The experts couldn't come to an agreement
Neither could the soul keepers

Can't make the mind work any longer
Shutting down the judicious clown
Sorry for the things said
Sincerely
    your letdown

Forever pay for this
Forever pay for that
What a shame it came to this
Don't want any pleasures

Swaying Palm Tree

A place for mischief was a synagogue
Behind the veil statues move
Who moved them?
     Not I
You spy with your all-seeing eye
     I lie
I was young
     I'm the swaying palm tree
I was a mischievous child
     please forgive me

Who's Zoo

The crocodile snaps
    for being paid in kind
The rhythm of the flop
    is far behind

The flamingo perches
    high on one leg
Under the sand hides
    the ostrich's head
And I say yeah
    maybe life will take on the colour of gold

Bluebirds of paradise
    are birds on a wing
Find the oasis
    join in and sing

The dyslexic is ruler
    when measuring foresight
They are mindless
    with unusual right
And I say yeah
    maybe life will take on the colour of gold

Giant kings of the circus ring
    rest in gory decay
Greed made them tuskless

for the rich to say
Yeah to the giant kings
    your ivory life will take on the colour of gold

When the maker snaps
    over those he's perched
It will be no paradise
    for manic is ruler
When standing in our ring
    fire will take on the colour of gold

We can amend

Tusk

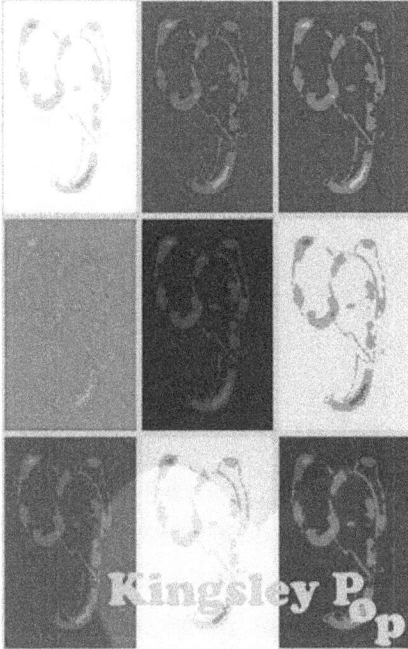

Trade of ivory illegal
Undeserving butchery
Sorrow
Kraft the heads of poachers
      upon spikes in multiple rows
      birds eat eyes of torturers
      an cnd–foreclose

We cannot take what doesn't belong to us
Retribution

Lovers Rust Together

Calling–concerning the heart–was granted
    it chanted
    angel wanted
To me you're the whole thing
    you're queen
    I'm king

Consent–concerning the soul–gave interweave
    never leave
    heavenly receive
To me you're the whole thing
    you're queen
    I'm king

What was has gone
      replaced with new
But what we hold dear
      will never die

The Secret

When the liquid changes its hue
The secret will be revealed to you

Under the rays of the burning sun
    bleaching the bones of everyone
Here we will wait for him to come
    being your answer the special one

Trust

Who to trust
When one takes
    and gives nothing back
When the other gives everything

Hold me
    for love casts out fear
I expire
I shall be released

The Shame of It All

Placing hands around a haunted head
Sorrowed face pressed against the wall
Roughness embedded
    layers shredded
Wishing hadn't said those vicious words
Oh his shame
    his shame of it all
Blood felt as rain

Bricks are warming to sky's crying
Blooded face pressed against the wall
Stickiness stings
    hateful thing
Loss of face as always moderates
Oh what shame
    what shame of it all
Light felt as affection

Under the ever so bright light
A photograph justifying against the appall
Who sees
    bending knees
Oh the shame
    the shame of it all
Peace felt as thieving

Verily I say unto thee
    today shalt thou be with me in paradise–Luke 23:43

Sinner! Who Me?

A kiss so sweet
     will heal all sins
Lips so fresh
     crash as waves
Cleansing the sinner
Needed are angels

Lonesome Truly

A lonesome tree dies
No other trees weep
No lies

From the earth it grew
A lonesome tree falls
No review

No other trees care
To the earth it returns
No fare

Lonesome by far

Imaginary Friends

Hello, Arthur
Hi, Burrton
Yo, Gruvel
Greetings, Mary
G'day, little wolf

Hey, Kingsley
Hey there, Patrick
Keep rocking, Lucretia
Looking good, Humph
Meow, cat
Oh hi, Snup-snup, there you are!

Fill your head with thought so clear
     that friends believe in you
The night is for dreaming
The day sees the actuality
     my imaginary friends
Forasmuch as dreams are life

Be your wavelength

L
 say Hi

G
 say Hi

B
 say Hi

T
 be you
 say Hi

Q
 question away
 but please understand I find the word queer to be 70s offensive

And
H
 say Hi

All are welcome
 all are equal
 in this rainbow world

We Are

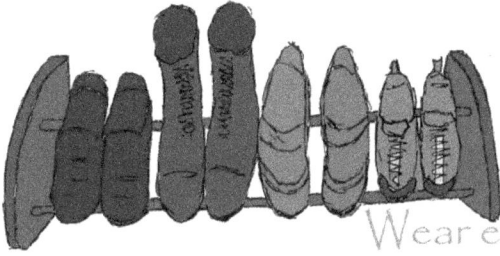

Wear the shoe which fits you
Be yourself
    be proud
      there's no need to sing out loud
Be your inner view

All are a point on a graphic image
Move beyond vintage
Visage

Stardust

We are created from stardust
We are sparkly
    light
    and we will live
We are opaque
    night
    yet we live
We all die

We are decayed to stardust
We are the dead
    around
    and we will live
We are the reborn
    bound
    yet we live
We are stardust

Levels of learning are your stairway
    as those who teach give the choice
    to live again
    to understand
    to endure
    to die
    to be whole
    to climb
    to be as one
    Stardust

Stardust

Each stardust grain existed afore the Earth was formed
It's been confirmed
      so are we programmed?
From the far-flung reaches of the universe came stardust
Like Earth
      inner is our central core
      our skin is its crust
Every piece of us is made from elements
      forged by stars
      sweet sentiments
But how was the soul forged?

Other

If ever a man should be judged
    then let it be on his love for the children of this world
    for they are the future
Our bodies are gone but our love remains
    eternally whispering amidst the trees

That's why tears are shed
    to keep your heart from becoming hard
    and crumbling to dust

Be strong
    keep a good heart
    for life is whatever you make it

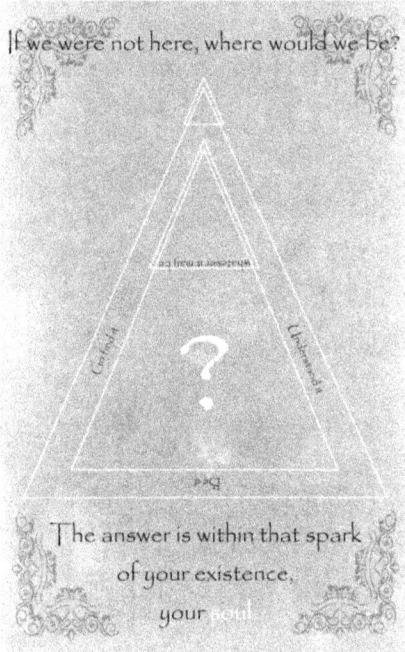

If we were not here
     where would we be?
The answer is within that spark of your existence
     your soul
Go find it
     understand it
     be it
Whatever it may be
?

Transcend

In the dark of my head
    waits a solitary bed
Where I can lay
    and rest halfway

Lead me blindfold
    across the threshold
To the new
    where I'm cut in two

If a ghost shows
    be it in shadows
If a friend appears
    God disperse my fears

In this reality
    body is absentee
Take my hand
    and transcend
    don't be inane
    walk to those you have lost and found again

Increment

You are free
      from the body tree
Let your soul rise
      in increment reprise

Sky of Stars

Let the sky of stars shine upon this earth of ours
and let all its children be as colourful as flowers

Colourful Flowers

The light in some burn brightly
      the light in some just burn
The light of some are beyond our mortal vision
      their light one day to return

All are in hearts
      for we are of the stars

Black on the outside
White on the outside
Close your eyes to the packaging
      for beauty and ugly can stand side by side
      and the same within

And Did Those Feet

The water in the photo is the man-made lake in Pickering Park, Kingston upon Hull. It's strange looking at it, remembering all those faces. This was a Stickleback-interest-day, just a stone's throw from Bethune Junior School.

At my senior school, Kingston High, I was made to run around this lake. I'd pretend to be Tom Courtenay from The Loneliness of the Long Distance Runner and sing Jerusalem: And did those feet in ancient time, walk upon England's mountains green? Incidentally, Sir Tom also went to Kingston. I possibly ran his path around that lake: And did my feet in school time, run upon Tom's footprints unseen? Non sibi cunctis–Not for oneself but for all.

My dad told me he used to swim in the lake when he was a child–he'd jump in, swim around, and climb out from the slope I'm stood on. So where am I in the photo? I'm third from the front.

I remember sunlight on this water. I used to row a boat there during the summer holidays–Come in number 7 your time is up. I also recall how cold it was when I fell into it. In winter, I'd skate upon its iced surface. It was exciting, but dangerous–non cotton wool days. If only there was a way to travel back in time. If simply for the purpose of putting your wrongs to right–enough said.

Sincerely,
Lawrence

L. Sydney Abel

And did those feet in ancient time
*   walk upon England's mountains green?*

From a short poem by William Blake

Our Journey

Some journeys are short
    others are long
We have no say in the amount of time we have on our journey
All journeys are different
    just like those who go on journeys

Everywhere is your garden my friend
Wherever the flowers bend
For evermore

Loser

Please cut my strings
     tell me things
Hold me
     don't let me fall
I'm so very small
I know nothing at all

I'm not sure if I cried tears of joy or sadness after the telling time
Truth is I've always been this of which I am
Nothing more and nothing less
A head full of something wonderful and distress

For Whom the Bells Toll

Hello
Perchance a birth that's pleasing
Perchance an adolescence seen emancipating
Perchance to marital to offspring
    given son
    given daughter
Perchance walking on calm water

Uncertainty in together in aging
Uncertainty with temper that's raging
Uncertainty if grandchild is shadow
    shallow genetics
    exhibiting traits
Uncertainty for whom the bells waits

Goodbye
Expiration from disease from killing
Expiration of body seen deteriorating
Expiration too insubstantial to dispose
    to bury
    or cremate
Expiration from where we originate

Life should be that wonderful dream
    nothing in between
Life
    one second

one minute
one hour
one day
one week
one month
one year
or more
Life is whatever
A life of flowing tears

For whom the bells toll

Toll

Tear us from our strife
Toll
      church bell ringing for the dead
Many are called gods by fame fed
Only one is all things as we are one
Father and son
Toll
      church bell
Toll
      church hell
Ringing in our head
      ringing for the dead
Torn is our life

A Larkin Toad (a writer's woe)

Writings will always be open to criticism

Criticism is never taken lightly
    when words are spat from mortal form
Hear the wily
    how they drone

Its three feet tall and four feet wide
And wherever you look it can manage to hide
A Larkin Toad can slip under the door
Like a green fog creeping over your floor
Or appear from a pinpoint of light
To give you the most terrible fright

Larkin Toad can guff
Trump
Let rip
Fart
And pump

The noise it makes will zip up your mouth
Making it difficult to laugh or even to shout
This windy-bottom toad visits day or night
So hold your nose ever so tight
If your verses shine
    there's no worry
If they're dull then hide in a hurry

A silent one or a squeak or an almighty blast
The smell is horrendous and wow does it last

Larkin Toad can guff
Trump
Let rip
Fart
And pump

If on the other hand you write as yourself
With no objective to be upon the popular shelf
Take your position
    bend and fart back
Pebbledash the toads who do the attack
The critical toads are a farce
Let them disappear up their own arse

Review (tongue in cheek)

Ribbit! Ribbit!
The worst I've read
Crap! Crap! Crap!
Didn't understand a word said

Brilliant!
It had me in tears
Utter garbage!
Don't give up the day job–herald by cheers

A bad critic's arse is a mouthpart
A bow is backward
Giving raspberry tart
Place the shit review in the toilet
Soil it
Can't spoil it–flush it–get over it

Death of An Actor

Who's been walking through the strangest places?
Who's been talking to many strange faces?
Who know what who's going through?
Who know what who's to do?
The death of an actor
Who could have carved your face in stone?
Who in the shadow of your beauty would be thrown?
Who wrote poems and poems for you?
Who is the wounded?
The death of an actor
Who draws lines on their face with life's fears?
Who played Romeo for a thousand years?
Who is the faceless actor?
Who is the undemonstrative adapter?

Horses for courses

Rental

My eyes are two lines from my 405 TV
X-rays are blinding me
Thinking absentee
      when dropping from the monkey tree
Vision is rental

After All

After all
    time is time
    it doesn't materially change
People change
    fashions change
    and seasons change
But time keeps the same
    simply passing

The Mind has Inconsistent Thoughts

One true thought
        or whatever I wish to call it
        is to the one I gave my love–my worship doesn't change

I will always see the blue in your eyes

Accept

Holler

at the

moon

before you drown
clown

accept

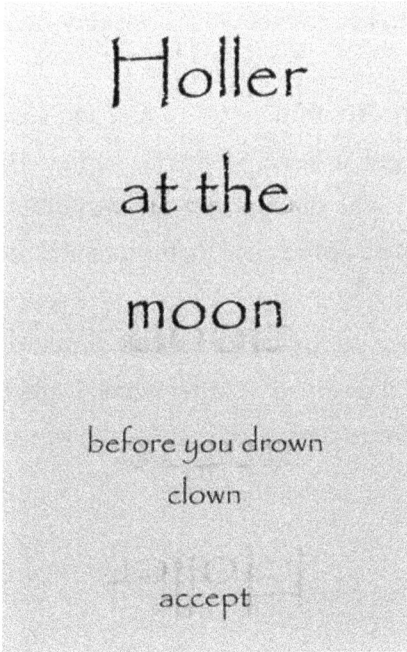

Death came that April Sunday
Death came that March Monday
Eyes I softly closed
My hurt is bitter
     my tongue is a fire

We're together in dreams

Time cannot remove my loss
Nor do the tears wash
Only a veil between us
Heart does clearly rip
     tears do silently drip

The young man with his hand in his pocket would one day save my life.

Drink and angst don't mix. A bedroom window, a fist, and seconds later a gash wide enough to reveal a severed artery gaped. Blood sprayed. Luckily my Uncle Keith was downstairs. A tourniquet and passing out several times saw me in an ambulance. In the hospital theatre I received a multitude of stitches.

I bare a jagged two-inch scar across my wrist. I'm not proud of my actions. I worried the ones I loved, and ruined a carpet which I splattered red. I could have died if it wasn't for my favourite uncle–the life saver.

Life Saver

A man of character
    upon life's soapbox
    with an opinionated voice
A description approx–a life saver
His life to rejoice
Memorable smacks received for bad behavior

All Emotions are Experienced

Sadness
    pain
    and grief is there
And the reason we feel those emotions is because of love
It's nothing to feel ashamed of
Love is one of the hardest things to explain
It's different for everyone
The feeling we have when we lose someone is so painful
    we think the world will never be the same again
Time is what's needed
Time is a wonderful healer
It doesn't remove pain
    it allows you to accept loss
When you can do that
    the pain will eventually disappear
It's replaced by sadness
And we can all live with sadness
    just the way we all live with happiness
The thing is to try and enjoy our happiness
    and reflect only for a short time on our sadness
Love is the reason
Without it
    it would be an empty world

Raw Ingredients

Nothing can be made without the raw ingredients
Sometimes all you need is a mind explosion
Think disobedience
Take the notion

Inking the Sky for Eternity

Inking the sky for eternity
Never carelessly
          but artfully
Dreams of the sweetest kind
Forever my conscious mind

The many that have become faceless
The many who can't be remembered
The many whose names I never knew
Where your kisses really so sweet?

Death's Beauty Lies

How fragrant you smell
    rotting in unmatched beauty
    to admire you is my duty
Hair lustrous by your side
    shimmering in red's blackness
    gaping slash now your necklace
How I cut
    with tongue's sharpness
    lost now in the dark abyss
Words are my way
    spoken still upon deaf ears
    love now forever appears

Brutal

The Future

Floating

Nothing can be done about the past but to visit
      to reminisce and reflect
The current time isn't any better because the present…
      too late it's gone
The big event is the future and that is for us all
The future is our demise
And that's all there is without disguise
      we can reprise on the next level
The future is our end

Beautiful to Look Upon

One way or the other
    my sister
    my brother
    you're going
Whichever way the wind is blowing
Your tears
    flowing
Isn't life forgoing?
If only life was knowing

The winds carry you to the four corners of the earth
Truthful in their decision to deposit feelings
    lest not to contaminate those that seek their own inspiration
    for you are beautiful to look upon

Time

Time is the past, present and future. Time has a habit of eating age and spitting out youth, or vice versa.

TIME...

> this something
> is somewhat
> manipulating something
> everywhere

Plucked Early

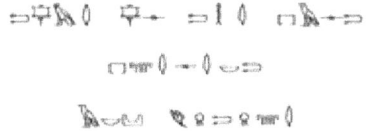

Reason made it so you couldn't see this world
Rooted was Death's grip
        refusing to let a beautiful girl unfurl

I think of you still
        sometimes tears spill
        sometimes I see your pain
        sometimes I refrain and see your beauty again
I see the little girl all grown up and looking down
        at her godfather clown
        who doesn't understand what you've come to learn
        as I'm not your concern
You are whatever will be
        but always Lindsey

I'd like to go back in time. My advice: make time for the ones
you love.

Nods

My soul tells my brain to listen
Response; my head nods in appreciation
    to those who fill my heart

Profound thanks to Kurt Mueller and Erica Mueller for all their hard work.

To the one who is always right from the one who is always wrong; your skills have been invaluable–love always.

An accolade for never-ending love and support goes to my daughter Leanne.

To my son Christian, I thank him for not arguing about my life's chapter of writing.

To Gerald, I thank him for the truth–brothers forever.

Thanks to Carly McCracken for saying the door is always open.

Additional thanks to Veronica Castle, and again to Carly McCracken for their combined ideas of books for charity–they are collections of stories donated by authors, where all profits go to a specified charity. I feel privileged to have contributed to such worthy causes.

Esteem goes to those of whom I have fond memories.
Family members on my mother's side:

Uncle Keith and Auntie Jean: for being the best ever.
Uncle Clive: for the American baseball hat.
Great Aunt Clarice: for her love and acceptance.
Great Aunt Madge: for words of kindness.
Lynn Evans: for helping me up when I'd fallen down.
Great Uncle Stan: for the crazy Christmas Caroling.
Val & Harry Bolder: for the up-to-date information on David Bowie and the Spiders from Mars, and for the discounted records.
Trevor Bolder: for his brilliant bass playing and kind words.

There are too many fond memories of my 1st cousins to name here; they will remain in my head till they fade into the cosmos. Those wonderful individuals (named alphabetically, so no favouritism here) are: Cheryl, Christine, Christopher, Clive, David, Ivor, Julian, Linda, Pam, Philip, Royston and Wendy.

Family members on my father's side:
Grandma Mary: for the oranges.
Aunt Minnie: for the unnerving bumps in the night.
My Godfather Humphrey: for standing with us, supporting Hull City A.F.C.

Special thanks to Kev Cooper and Rik Lane.

For those who are not named, you are not yet forgotten. You are simply too many. Thank you all for enriching my life, one way or the other.

In lunacy of it all

Sign up for free and bargain books

Join the Speaking Volumes mailing list

Text

ILOVEBOOKS

to 22828 **to get started.**

Message and data rates may apply.

www.ingramcontent.com/pod-product-compliance
Lightning Source LLC
LaVergne TN
LVHW011233080426
835509LV00005B/482